## ALSO BY LIZ CLIMO

# a little book for mothers

(and the people who love them)

## liz climo

HarperCollins*Publishers*

HarperCollins*Publishers*
1 London Bridge Street
London SE1 9GF

www.harpercollins.co.uk

First published by Flatiron Books
This UK edition published by HarperCollins*Publishers* 2020

1 3 5 7 9 10 8 6 4 2

© Liz Climo 2020

Liz Climo asserts the moral right to be identified as the author of this work

A catalogue record of this book is available from the British Library

ISBN 978-0-00-840204-4

Designed by Steven Seighman

Printed and bound in Latvia

**MIX**
Paper from
responsible sources
**FSC™ C007454**

This book is produced from independently certified FSC™ paper to ensure responsible forest management.

For more information visit: www.harpercollins.co.uk/green

*For Marlow and Mary Lou*

# You're mum.

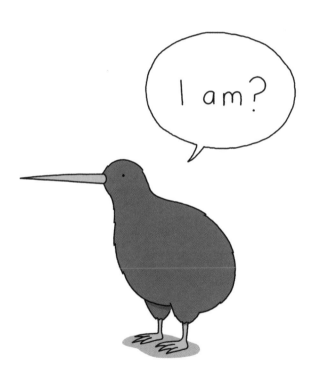

Maybe not! But you probably know a mum or a mum figure – and right now, I want to say thanks to all the mums out there. Specifically, the mums who are doing the best they can.

Full disclosure: I am a mum, but I didn't write this book about myself. (Can you imagine? *Hey everyone, aren't I the BEST? Go me!*) Yes, many of the jokes in here are based on my own experiences as a mum, but the idea for the book came from somewhere else.

Something significant happened when I became a mum (I mean, aside from not sleeping for about four months straight): It made me appreciate and feel more connected to my own mum, who died when I was twenty-two. I wrote this book for her, because she was wonderful. She wasn't perfect, of course. Like most mums, she made some mistakes and probably felt like she was doing a terrible job most of the time, but she loved her children unconditionally. She made us feel safe, and not just us – she opened her heart and door to other children who didn't feel love in their own homes. There are so many people out there like her, and if someone gave this book to you, you're probably one of them.

One of the hardest things about losing my mum at a young age was that everyone else seemed to still have their mums. That feeling of isolation lasted beyond the initial shock and heartache of losing her, and it became even more difficult after I had my own daughter. It felt so cruel that they would never get to know each other. When I was pregnant, I'd often wonder if my baby would look like her. I secretly hoped that my child's arrival would, in some way, bring my own mother back.

Then my daughter was born – with sparkly blue eyes and strawberry blond hair. She was lovely, but she didn't look a thing like my mum (or me, for that matter). She didn't really act like her, either. But that was okay! She is an entirely different person, after all.

Soon, I began to notice something: I'd catch a glimpse of my reflection in the mirror, and see my sleepy eyes and messy dark hair. I'd hear how I spoke to my daughter, or hear myself making up silly songs for her. I'd notice the way she made me laugh – a booming, unabashed laugh that I hadn't experienced in ages. And I could feel how much my daughter loved me. I recognized that feeling because I felt the same way about my own mum. Rather than seeing my mum in my daughter, I had started to see my mum in myself.

Does that mean we feel that sort of connection to our parents only when we have children of our own? Nope! That was just how I happened to get to that place – but what do I know? (Just kidding. I'm very wise. Please don't put this book down.) Some of us have children, and some of us don't. Some of us have wonderful relationships with our parents, and some of us don't. I don't want this book to be some secret handbook that only mums are allowed to have. Rather, I want to acknowledge those people out there doing the difficult and often very lonely job of being a parent, or being in a parental role. You are doing incredible things for the people who are lucky enough to be loved by you.

My own mum taught me the importance of unconditional love, acceptance, generosity, and kindness. I am grateful for all of you out there doing the same, either with your own children or just the people you surround yourself with. You make the world a much better place, and this book is for you.

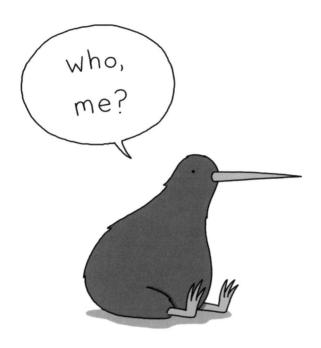

Yes, you. I still think you're great, by the way, whether or not you're mum.

Thanks. I hope you like it.

Liz

You're mum.

You've had to read a lot of picture books.

only this many more.

(And if you haven't already,
you will soon. I promise.)

So, here's a picture
book just for you.

Becoming a mum is a pretty big deal.

Sometimes, it happens fast.

Sometimes, it takes a while.

Sometimes, it feels like you've been waiting forever.

8

Sometimes, it's a big surprise.

However it happens . . .

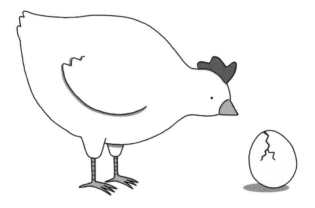

. . . this incredible journey has just begun.

Today's the day.
Your little one is finally here,

and she's perfect.

This precious gift is yours
to love forever.

How lucky are you?

Sure, having a new baby can be
a little intimidating at first.

Okay . . . a lot intimidating.

Sometimes, you connect immediately.

Sometimes, you don't.

(Which is perfectly normal, by the way.)

These early weeks can be challenging.
Luckily, everyone has plenty
of advice for you.

omg. he is adorable. how old? he doesn't sleep in there, does he? just make sure you don't smother him. is he hungry? he seems hungry. You have to feed him every two hours, or he'll die. and you should take him out of there sometimes so his head doesn't get too flat. does his head look flat to you? my cousin's baby had a flat hea—

Remember sleep?

Well, you won't.

There will also be mood swings . . .

. . . and not much
time to yourself.

You may not recognize
yourself for a while.

Sometimes, you may even feel
you've lost a little bit of yourself.

This part may feel like it will last forever, but it won't.

Days
without
Sleep
卌 卌 卌
卌 卌 卌
卌 卌 卌
|||

One day, the infant phase will end . . .

. . . and she may start to talk . . .

. . . and she may never . . .

. . . ever . . .

. . . stop.

Remember when you
thought having a newborn
was hard?

Wait until you have a toddler.

There will be a lot of questions.

Seriously, a
LOT.

And there will be plenty of fun.

Before you know it,
your baby will be a kid . . .

(You know what I mean.)

. . . and he may start to
become more independent.

There will be some
embarrassing moments.

(For both of you.)

There will also be
learning moments.

(For both of you.)

Soon, you'll have a teenager.

THEY'RE FUN!

There will be disagreements . . .

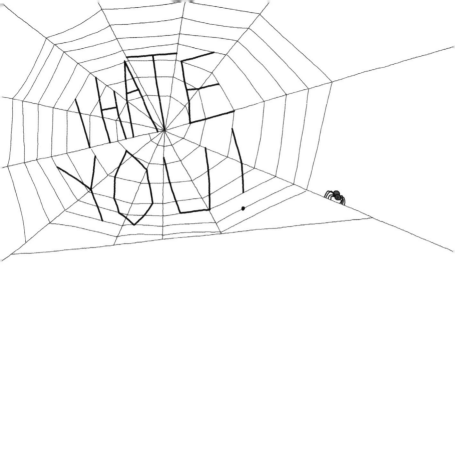

. . . and plenty of drama.

But there will
also be late-night
conversations . . .

. . . and laughter . . .

. . . and lots . . .

... and lots ...

. . . of love.

Where has the time gone?

It seems like only a month ago,
he was a chick.

(You know what I mean.)

This part is hard.

But you aren't alone!

And you can handle it.

After all, mums have been doing
this for millions of years.

And there are billions of other mums
out there, in all shapes and sizes.

There are younger mums.

And older mums.

Mums who look like their kids.

And mums who don't.

There are grandparents who are mums.

Cousins, sisters, and
friends who are mums.

Stepmums and foster mums.

Mums who have yearned.

And mums who have lost.

Some families have more than one mum.

Or a parent who takes on the role of mum.

There are mums
who go to work.

And mums who stay home.

(They're working, too!)

Mums who have help.

Mums who do it alone.

Mums who never leave their kids alone.

Mums who leave much too soon.

This part is hard.

But mums never *really* leave.

Because your words . . .

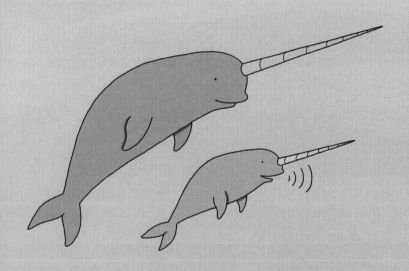

. . . become her words.

Your lessons . . .

. . . become his lessons.

Your love . . .

. . . becomes her love.

Because there is no
love as powerful . . .

. . . as a mother's love.

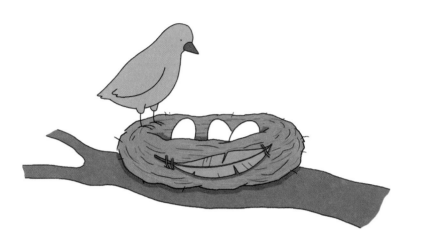

And that never goes away.

But seriously, if you have a baby joining your house soon, get some sleep now – like, RIGHT now. While you still can!

Trust me, you'll need your rest.

Because you're mum.

And there is no job on earth . . .

. . . more important than yours.

# Acknowledgments

I would like to say thanks to whoever is holding this book right now. Whether you've seen my work before or are looking at it now for the first time, thank you so much for your support. To Kathleen Ortiz, and everyone at New Leaf Literary, for their continuous hard work. Sarah Murphy, and everyone at Flatiron Books, for believing in this project and helping me realize the vision for it. To my family and friends, who helped give me feedback on this book in its early stages, and who helped inspire much of its content. My brother, sister, and dad, for their constant and continuous support. My husband, who I am so lucky to have as both a partner and friend, and who is always willing to give honest, creative feedback. To my mom, who taught me what unconditional love is, and my daughter, who reminds me what it is every day.

# About the Author

LIZ CLIMO grew up in the San Francisco Bay Area and moved to Los Angeles after college to work as a character artist on *The Simpsons*. She started the popular Instagram comic series *The Little World of Liz Climo* at @lizclimo, which became her debut comic collection. She is also the author and illustrator of several comics and children's books. Liz currently lives in Los Angeles with her husband and their daughter.